ExamREVIEW.NET

Intellectual Properties, Trademarks and Copyrights

Contents of this book are fully copyrighted. We develop study material entirely on our own. Braindump is strictly prohibited. This book comes with LIFE TIME FREE UPDATES. When you find a newer version, all you need to do is to go and download. **Please check our web site's Free Updates section regularly:**

http://www.examreview.net/free_updates.htm

The Book

We create these self-practice test questions module (with 120+ questions) referencing both the technical concepts and state specific information currently valid in the elevator trade. Each question comes with an answer and a short explanation which aids you in seeking further study information. For purpose of exam readiness drilling, this product includes questions that have varying numbers of choices. Some have 2 while some have 5 or 6. We want to make sure these questions are tough enough to really test your readiness and draw your focus to the weak areas. **You should use this product together with other study resources for the best possible exam prep coverage.**

Table of Contents (Elevator – Connecticut)

Question 1:

Which device prevents the elevator from overspeeding?

Possible Choices:

governor

cylinder

cartop lock

piston

hoistway

interlock

Answer:

It is the governor that prevents the elevator from overspeeding. If the elevator overspeeds, the governor device will pull on the safety device and stop the car.

Question 2:

Hoist cables are usually made of:

Possible Choices:

ropes

strong fiber belt

iron

steel cables

interlocked cables

Answer:

Hoist cables are strong steel cables made of individual high strength flexible steel wires. Traction elevators usually come with at least 4 of these cables.

Question 3:

The structure that surrounds the elevator is known as:

Possible Choices:

cylinder

cartop

carrack

racktop

piston

hoistway

Answer:

Hoistway is the structure that surrounds the elevator. It is supposed to be fire resistant enclosure.

Question 4:

A safety device can quickly stop an elevator when:

Possible Choices:

it moves in the up direction too fast

it moves in the down direction too fast

it moves in any direction too fast

Answer:

A safety device can quickly stop an elevator when it moves in the down direction too fast or when the ropes are suddenly broken. It uses a jaw like mechanism to forcefully grip the rails.

Question 5:

The pump unit includes (choose all that apply):

Possible Choices:

oil tank

motor

pump

valve

None of the choices.

Answer:

The pump unit is the power unit of a hydraulic elevator. It has a reservoir oil tank, a motor together with the pump and valve.

Question 6:

With a hydraulic elevator, when the oil tank of the pump unit is low on oil,

<u>Possible Choices:</u>

the elevator may have difficulties getting to the top floor.

the elevator may have difficulties getting to the lower floors.

the cut off level my be triggered.

the interlock may freeze.

Answer:

With a hydraulic elevator, when the oil tank of the pump unit is low on oil, the elevator may have difficulties getting to the top floor.

Question 7:

Fire recall circuitry is required in most commercial setups.

True

False

Answer:

True. Fire recall circuitry can send an elevator to a designated floor during a fire. It is required in most commercial setups.

Question 8:

For elevators installed in flood hazard areas, the designated floor should be located:

Possible Choices:

below the BFE

above the BFE.

Answer:

For elevators installed in flood hazard areas, the designated floor should be located above the Base Flood Elevation BFE whenever possible.

Question 9:

When an elevator is for providing access to areas below the Base Flood Elevation BFE, it should come with:

Possible Choices:

a float switch system.

a passive switch system.

a fixed switch system.

Answer:

When an elevator is for providing access to areas below the Base Flood Elevation BFE, it should come with a float switch system.

Question 10:

Traction elevators usually come with at least how many hoist cables?

Possible Choices:

2

3

4

5

6

Answer:

Hoist cables are strong steel cables made of individual high strength flexible steel wires. Traction elevators usually come with at least 4 of these cables.

Question 11:

Practically speaking, emergency power generators should be required for elevators of:

Possible Choices:

2 stories or greater.

4 stories or greater.

10 stories or greater.

12 stories or greater.

15 stories or greater.

Answer:

Emergency power generators should be required for elevators of 4 stories or greater.

Question 12:

Hydraulic elevators are either:

Possible Choices:

direct acting or holeless.

indirect acting or holeful.

indirect acting or holeless.

active acting or passive acting.

Answer:

Hydraulic elevators are either direct acting or holeless.

Question 13:

Vertical platform lifts VPLs are either:

Possible Choices:

direct or indirect.

stepped or continuous.

active or passive.

open or fully enclosed.

Answer:

Vertical platform lifts VPLs are either open or fully enclosed.

Question 14:

Traction elevator systems are most commonly installed in high-rise construction buildings.

Possible Choices:

True

False

Answer:

True. Traction elevator systems are most commonly installed in high-rise construction buildings.

Question 15:

Vertical platform lifts VPLs are for transporting:

Possible Choices:

heavy weight items.

oversized items.

individual in a wheelchair.

goods.

Answer:

Vertical platform lifts VPLs are for transporting individual in a wheelchair. A wheelchair bound person may enter the lift on one side and exit through another when the lift is equipped with 2 doors.

Question 16:

With a direct acting hydraulic elevator, there is a hydraulic jack assembly extending:

Possible Choices:

above the lowest floor covering the pit area.

below the lowest floor into the pit area.

below the highest floor above the pit area.

Answer:

With a direct acting hydraulic elevator, there is a hydraulic jack assembly extending below the lowest floor into the pit area.

Question 17:

In the context of traction elevators, what equipments are typically placed at the bottom of the elevator shaft (choose all that apply):

Possible Choices:

selector tapes

governor rope assembly

oil buffers

counterweight roller guides

compensation cable assembly

limit switches

Answer:

In the context of traction elevators, important equipments including counterweight roller guides, compensation cable assembly, limit switches, selector tapes, governor rope assembly, oil buffers ...etc are typically placed at the bottom of the elevator shaft.

Question 18:

When dealing with hoist ropes, grade may be expressed as tensile strength in N/mm2 or:

Possible Choices:

Psi

Lbs

Rbs

Cbt

Answer:

When dealing with hoist ropes, grade may be expressed as tensile strength in Newtons/square millimeter N/mm2 or pounds/square inch psi.

Question 19:

Chairlifts are designed to be used inside a structure.

Possible Choices:

True

False

Answer:

True. Chairlifts are installed over or alongside a staircase for transporting peoples between floors. They are designed to be used inside a structure only.

Question 20:

With a holeless hydraulic elevator, there is a cylinder in the shaft:

Possible Choices:

below the pit level.

above the pit level.

Answer:

With a holeless hydraulic elevator, there is a cylinder in the shaft above the pit level.

Question 21:

Which of these is supposed to be fire resistant enclosure?

Possible Choices:

cylinder

cartop

carrack

racktop

piston

hoistway

Answer:

Hoistway is the structure that surrounds the elevator. It is supposed to be fire resistant enclosure.

Question 22:

Elevator car doors must be fire rated.

Possible Choices:

True

False

Answer:

False. Most typical elevator doors have a 1 and 1/2 "B" label rating. On the other hand, elevator car doors may not be fire rated.

Question 23:

Hoist ropes are either:

Possible Choices:

Traction or Extra High Strength Traction

Traction or Extra High Flexibility Traction

Low Traction or High Traction

Answer:

Hoist ropes are either Traction or Extra High Strength Traction. Extra High Strength Traction rope is usually required for high-rise high-speed applications.

Question 24:

Hydraulic elevators are commonly found in:

Possible Choices:

low-rise construction buildings.

high-rise construction buildings.

high-rise commercial buildings.

Answer:

Hydraulic elevators are commonly found in low-rise construction buildings.

Question 25:

Which device is for counterbalancing the weight of the elevator car?

Possible Choices:

Interlock

Cartop

Racktop

Traction control

Counterweight

Answer:

Counterweight is for counterbalancing the weight of the elevator car. Simply put, when the elevator car goes up, the counterweight goes down, and vice versa.

Question 26:

The pump unit is the major power unit of a traction elevator.

Possible Choices:

Possible Choices:

True

False

Answer:

False. The pump unit is the power unit of a hydraulic elevator. It has a reservoir oil tank, a motor together with the pump and valve.

Question 27:

Stranding is all about:

the number of strands per rope

the number of wires per strand

the number of strands per rope as well as the number of wires per strand.

untwisting the rope

Answer:

Stranding is all about the number of strands per rope as well as the number of wires per strand. Do note that wire ropes have the propensity to untwist, which could weaken the rope structure. Untwisting of the ropes must be carefully prevented.

Question 28:

Preformed ropes are preferred due to what reason?

Possible Choices:

They can provide longer rope service life.

They are cheaper.

They are always coated.

Answer:

You should replace governor and compensation ropes with preformed ropes only. They can provide longer rope service life.

Question 29:

Elastic stretch describes:

Possible Choices:

the increase in rope length when there is no increase in load.

the increase in rope length when there is an increase in load.

the increase in rope length when untwisted.

Answer:

Elastic stretch describes the increase in rope length when there is an increase in load.

Question 30:

The lay of governor ropes is always:

Possible Choices:

Right Regular

Right Lang

Left Regular

Left Lang

Answer:

The lay of governor ropes is always Right Regular. The lay of compensation ropes is also always Right Regular.

Question 31:

In CT, which license is in fact an accessibility contractor's license?

Possible Choices:

R1

R2

R5

R6

Answer:

In CT, a Limited contractor elevator license R5 is in fact an accessibility contractor's license. The Limited journeyperson elevator license R6, on the other hand, is an accessibility journeyperson's license.

Question 32:

In CT, each elevator should be inspected by an elevator inspector at least:

Possible Choices:

once every 6 months.

once every 12 months.

once every 18 months.

once every 24 months.

once every 36 months.

Answer:

In CT, each elevator should be inspected by an elevator inspector at least once every eighteen months.

Question 1:

What keeps the hoistway door closed when the car is not at the current floor?

Possible Choices:

governor

cylinder

cartop lock

piston

hoistway

interlock

Answer:

An interlock keeps the hoistway door closed when the car is not at the current floor.

Question 2:

Elevator door entrance frames may not be fire rated.

Possible Choices:

True

False

Answer:

False. Most typical elevator doors have a 1 and 1/2 "B" label rating. Same for the elevator door entrance frames. On the other hand, elevator car doors may not be fire rated.

Question 3:

You should always replace compensation ropes with preformed ropes.

Possible Choices:

True

False

Answer:

True. You should replace governor and compensation ropes with preformed ropes only. You may look at the rope tag to figure out the breaking load.

Question 4:

With a traditional geared traction elevator system, there is an electric motor located:

Possible Choices:

above the elevator shaft.

below the elevator shaft.

inside the elevator shaft.

Answer:

Traditional geared traction elevator systems have cables connected to the top of the cab. There is an electric motor located above the elevator shaft.

Question 5:

Steel-reinforced natural fiber may be used ONLY in low-rise low-speed applications.

Possible Choices:

True

False

Answer:

False. Natural fiber is a very common choice of core used in elevator ropes. Steel-reinforced natural fiber or full steel core ropes may also be used in high-rise high-speed applications. When reverse bends are present, compacted strand wire rope may be used due to increased rope service life.

Question 6:

Galvanized coating on ropes is never allowed.

Possible Choices:

True

False

Answer:

False. Bright uncoated rope is the industry standard. For better protection you may want to use galvanized coating.

Question 7:

The crown wires do NOT make contact with the sheave.

Possible Choices:

True

False

Answer:

False. The crown wires make contact with the sheave. Eventually they will show signs of abrasion.

Question 8:

Traction elevators may be:

Possible Choices:

geared or gearless.

indirect or direct.

active or passive.

belt driven or chain driven.

Answer:

Traction elevators may be geared or gearless. The former are typically used for smaller low-rise structures. The latter are used for larger high-rise building structures.

Question 9:

Retaining clips are not supposed to bear any load.

Possible Choices:

True

False

Answer:

True. The retaining clips do not bear any load. You use them to keep the wedge in place when there is a momentary loss of load on the rope.

Question 10:

All out of the factory new elevator ropes come with a metal tag showing (choose all that apply):

Possible Choices:

diameter

breaking load

grade

construction classification

lubrication procedures

year of installation.

Answer:

All new elevator ropes come with a metal tag showing the diameter, breaking load, grade, construction classification, manufacturer and lubrication procedures. HOWEVER, it is the installer who needs to fill in information on the month and year of installation.

Question 11:

The governor rope requires very precise tensioning.

Possible Choices:

True

False

Answer:

False. Generally speaking, the governor rope would not require the precise tensioning needed by the hoist rope.

Question 12:

Generally, a rope lay is about _____ times the diameter of the rope.

Answer:

Generally, a rope lay is about 6.5 times the diameter of the rope.

Question 13:

Elevator wire ropes must be lubricated by the installer during first time installation.

Possible Choices:

True

False

Answer:

False. Generally speaking, all wire rope comes factory-lubricated. During maintenance, using automatic lubricators would be way more time-efficient.

Question 14:

The lay of compensation ropes is always:

Possible Choices:

Right Regular

Right Lang

Left Regular

Left Lang

Answer:

The lay of governor ropes is always Right Regular. The lay of compensation ropes is also always Right Regular.

Question 15:

Natural fiber is not allowed to be used in elevator ropes.

Possible Choices:

True

False

Answer:

False. Natural fiber is a very common choice of core used in elevator ropes. Steel-reinforced natural fiber or full steel core ropes may also be used in high-rise high-speed applications.

Question 16:

The valley wires do not have any contact with the sheave.

Possible Choices:

True

False

Answer:

True. The valley wires are in the valleys of two adjacent strands, without having any contact with the sheave.

Question 17:

When one rope of a set that has been subjected to elevator service requires replacement,

Possible Choices:

only the damaged rope needs to be replaced.

the entire set should be replaced.

Answer:

When one rope of a set that has been subjected to elevator service requires replacement, the entire set should be replaced.

Question 18:

When a rope requires replacement, the tension of the new replacement rope should be checked at semi-monthly intervals:

Possible Choices:

during the first month after installation.

during the first 2 months after installation.

during the first 3 months after installation.

during the first 6 months after installation.

during the first 9 months after installation.

Answer:

When a rope requires replacement, the tension of the new replacement rope should be checked at semi-monthly intervals during the first two months after installation.

Question 19:

Elevator pit depths commonly range between __ and __ feet for hydraulic elevators.

Possible Choices:

4/5

3/6

2/7

1/6

2/3

Answer:

Elevator pit depths commonly range between 4 and 5 feet for hydraulic elevators.

Question 20:

The replacement criteria for steel wire rope are always based on the least possible conditions of diameter and wire breaks.

Possible Choices:

True

False

Answer:

False. The replacement criteria for steel wire rope are always based on the worst possible conditions of diameter and wire breaks.

Question 21:

A breakaway wall is intended to serve as part of the structural support of the building.

Possible Choices:

True

False

Answer:

False. A breakaway wall is not part of the structural support of the building. It is intended to collapse under specific lateral loading forces without causing damage to other parts of the building.

Question 22:

Compacted strand wire rope may NEVER be used in any elevator conditions.

Possible Choices:

True

False

Answer:

False. Natural fiber is a very common choice of core used in elevator ropes. When reverse bends are present, compacted strand wire rope may be used due to increased rope service life.

Question 23:

Talking about fasteners, set screws or threaded portions located in the shear plane of bolts and screws may be used for transmitting load.

<u>Possible Choices:</u>

True

False

Answer:

False. Talking about fasteners, set screws or threaded portions located in the shear plane of bolts and screws should NEVER be used for transmitting load. Also, there should be no relative motion between those rigidly joined components that transmit load.

Question 24:

A base flood refers to a flood:

Possible Choices:

with 1-percent chance of being equaled or exceeded in any given year.

with 2-percent chance of being equaled or exceeded in any given year.

with 3-percent chance of being equaled or exceeded in any given year.

with 1-percent chance of being equaled or exceeded in any given year within 50 years.

with 1.5-percent chance of being equaled or exceeded in any given year within 50 years.

Answer:

A base flood refers to a flood with 1-percent chance of being equaled or exceeded in any given year. Many guidelines and NFIP regulations affect elevators.

Question 25:

Counterweights should be provided with guide rails.

Possible Choices:

True

False

Answer:

True. Counterweights should be provided with guide rails. They should be made of steel or other metal that conforms to the relevant requirements.

Question 26:

What refers to the elevation to which development in the regulatory floodplain is built?

Possible Choices:

BFE

CFE

DFE

GFE

GRA

Answer:

Design flood elevation DFE refers to the elevation to which development in the regulatory floodplain is built. Normally the minimum requirement for it is the BFE.

Question 27:

An accessible stop switch is always necessary for an elevator.

Possible Choices:

True

False

Answer:

True. A stop switch that is accessible from the point of access to the machinery spaces or control spaces should be made available for every elevator.

Question 28:

A seismic switch can signal:

Possible Choices:

rope breakage

an earthquake

a flood

a windstorm

Answer:

A seismic switch is a device that gets activated by ground movement. It can signal a potentially damaging earthquake.

Question 29:

What device can automatically cause electrical power to be removed from the elevator driving-machine motor when the suspension ropes of the winding drum machine turns slack?

Possible Choices:

slack-rope switch

interlock

cut off lever

safety catch

sight guard

Answer:

A slack-rope switch can automatically cause electrical power to be removed from the elevator driving-machine motor when the suspension ropes of the winding drum machine turns slack.

Question 30:

Elevator cars do not need metal guide rails.

<u>Possible Choices:</u>

True

False

Answer:

False. Elevator cars should be provided with guide rails. They should be made of steel or other metal that conforms to the relevant requirements.

Question 31:

In CT, a person must have served at least _____ years as an R-2 journeyperson or equivalent in order to earn an unlimited contractor elevator license R-1.

Possible Choices:

1

2

3

4

5

Answer:

In CT, a person must have served at least two years as an R-2 journeyperson or equivalent in order to earn an unlimited contractor elevator license R-1.

Question 32:

In CT, each private residence elevator should be inspected:

Possible Choices:

every 6 months.

every 9 months.

every 12 months.

every 24 months.

upon the request of the owner.

Answer:

In CT, each private residence elevator should be inspected upon the request of the owner.

Question 1:

Nonmetallic materials may be used as guide rails if the rated speed of the car does not go over:

Possible Choices:

0.75 m/s.

1.75 m/s.

2.75 m/s.

3.75 m/s.

4.75 m/s.

5.75 m/s.

Answer:

In certain hazardous condition, nonmetallic materials may be used as guide rails if the rated speed of the car does not go over 0.75 m/s.

Question 2:

What device can reduce the opening that situates between the leading edges of the hoistway door and the car door?

Possible Choices:

slack-rope guard

interlocking guard

cut off guard

safety guard

sight guard

Answer:

A sight guard is mounted on the hoistway side of the leading edge of the hoistway door. It can reduce the opening that situates between the leading edges of the hoistway door and the car door.

Question 3:

Elevator pit depths commonly range between __ and __ feet for traction elevators.

Possible Choices:

1/3

2/5

4/7

6/8

7/9

Answer:

Elevator pit depths commonly range between 6 and 8 feet for traction elevators.

Question 4:

A _____ door is a door that pivots around a vertical axis.

Possible Choices:

swinging

vertical sliding

horizontal sliding

Answer:

A swinging door is a door that pivots around a vertical axis.

Question 5:

A horizontally sliding collapsible gate has horizontally sliding horizontal members that are joined by a chain link style linkage.

Possible Choices:

True

False

Answer:

False. A horizontally sliding collapsible gate has horizontally sliding vertical members that are joined by a scissors-style linkage. This linkage is designed to allow the assembly to collapse.

Question 6:

A semiautomatic gate is designed to be opened automatically and closed manually when the car leaves the landing.

<u>Possible Choices:</u>

True

False

Answer:

False. A semiautomatic gate is designed to be opened manually and closed automatically when the car leaves the landing.

Question 7:

What describe the distance in step lengths the leading edge of the escalator step travels once emerged from the comb but before making any vertical movement?

Unit steps

Forward steps

Flat steps

Trip steps

Answer:

Flat steps describe the distance in step lengths the leading edge of the escalator step travels once emerged from the comb but before making any vertical movement.

Question 8:

A gate closer is a device that closes a gate via gravity ONLY.

Possible Choices:

True

False

Answer:

False. A gate closer is a device that closes a gate via means such as spring or gravity.

Question 9:

Moving walk represents:

the rate of travel with rated load on it.

the rate of travel without rated load on it.

Answer:

Moving walk represents the rate of travel with rated load on it.

Question 10:

A dumbwaiter is a hoisting and lowering mechanism that is equipped with a car of limited size for carrying:

Possible Choices:

materials.

human and materials.

fluids.

Answer:

A dumbwaiter is a hoisting and lowering mechanism that is equipped with a car of limited size for carrying materials.

Question 11:

For a reversible inclined moving walks, the rated speed represents the rate of travel that:

Possible Choices:

goes up and with rated load on it.

goes up and without rated load on it.

goes down and with rated load on it.

goes down and without rated load on it.

Answer:

For a reversible inclined moving walks, the rated speed represents the rate of travel that goes up and with rated load on it.

Question 12:

An access panel should be kept opened at all time.

Possible Choices:

True

False

Answer:

False. An access panel should be kept closed and locked all the time. However, it should NOT be self-closing.

Question 13:

For maintenance use, a working platform should be able to support minimum _____ lb in any position.

Possible Choices:

150

200

250

300

350

400

450

Answer:

For maintenance use, a working platform should be able to support minimum 450 lb in any position.

Question 14:

Permanent electric lighting in all machinery spaces should have illumination which is no less than
_____ lx at the floor level.

Possible Choices:

50

90

100

120

150

180

200

Answer:

Permanent electric lighting should be available in all machinery spaces and control rooms, with
illumination no less than 200 lx at the floor level.

Question 15:

Equipments NOT for use directly with the elevator:

Possible Choices:

should be disallowed in elevator hoistways.

may still be allowed in elevator hoistways.

Answer:

Only equipments for use directly with the elevator are allowed in elevator hoistways.

Question 16:

Material lifts that have no automatic transfer devices are either:

Possible Choices:

Type I or Type II

Type A or Type B

Type S or Type F

Type C or Type H

Answer:

Material lifts that have no automatic transfer devices are either Type A or Type B. Note that Type A Material Lifts may only be controlled from landing-mounted operated devices.

Question 17:

Open power-operated doors should be designed to be closed only through continuous pressure imposed on the door close button.

Possible Choices:

True

False

Answer:

True. Open power-operated doors should be designed to be closed only through continuous pressure imposed on the door close button. Also, on a car that has multiple entrances, when multiple entrances can be opened at the same landing then there should be a separate door close button for each entrance.

Question 18:

Generally speaking, emergency doors are required even when there are no car safeties provided.

Possible Choices:

True

False

Answer:

False. Generally speaking, emergency doors are required only when there are car safeties provided.

Question 19:

Plunger gripper is never intended for use with direct-acting hydraulic elevators.

Possible Choices:

True

False

Answer:

False. A plunger gripper should be provided for direct-acting hydraulic elevators. It should be able to stop and hold the car with its rated load.

Question 20:

Type ____ Material Lifts may only be controlled from landing-mounted operated devices.

Possible Choices:

A

I

C

II

D

There is no such limitation.

Answer:

Material lifts that have no automatic transfer devices are either Type A or Type B. Type A Material Lifts may only be controlled from landing-mounted operated devices. Type B Material Lifts may carry one operator only.

Question 21:

A plunger gripper is supposed to mechanically or electrically grip the plunger.

Possible Choices:

True

False

Answer:

False. Plunger gripper is supposed to mechanically grip the plunger. Hydraulic means may be used to hold the gripper in a retracted position.

Question 22:

A governor rope should be no less than ___ mm in diameter.

Possible Choices:

3

4

5

6

7

8

9

Answer:

A governor rope should be made of iron, steel, or metal no less than 6 mm in diameter. Keep in mind, tiller-rope construction should never be used.

Question 23:

A device that measures load should be allowed to prevent operation of the elevator below the required capacity.

Possible Choices:

True

False

Answer:

False. A device that measures load should not be allowed to prevent operation of the elevator at or below the required capacity and loading.

Question 24:

On a car that has multiple entrances, when multiple entrances can be opened at the same landing then there should be one close button that can control all the entrances.

Possible Choices:

True

False

Answer:

False. On a car that has multiple entrances, when multiple entrances can be opened at the same landing then there should be a separate door close button for each entrance.

Question 25:

Type B Material Lifts may carry max how many operators?

Possible Choices:

0

1

2

There is no such limit.

Answer:

Material lifts that have no automatic transfer devices are either Type A or Type B. Note that Type B Material Lifts may carry one operator only.

Question 26:

When an elevator car stops at a landing, all the registered car calls for that landing:

Possible Choices:

should be canceled.

should be retained.

Answer:

When an elevator car stops at a landing, all the registered car calls for that landing should be canceled.

Question 27:

Terminal speed reducing device is always implemented via mechanical means.

Possible Choices:

True

False

Answer:

False. When a terminal speed reducing device is implemented via electrical means, a single short circuit caused by a combination of conditions should not be able to make the device ineffective.

Question 28:

Electrohydraulic elevators may have multiple means to control upward movement but:

Possible Choices:

one of these should be controlled by the terminal speed reducing device.

none of these should be controlled by the terminal speed reducing device.

Answer:

Electrohydraulic elevators may have two means to control upward movement, such as pump motor and valve. One or both of these should be controlled by the terminal speed reducing device directly or indirectly.

Question 29:

For the sake of safety a plunger gripper when installed should stop functioning when there is a primary electrical system power failure.

Possible Choices:

True

False

Answer:

False. A plunger gripper when installed should remain fully operational even when there is a primary electrical system power failure.

Question 30:

Elevator movement controlled by terminal speed reducing device may be implemented with a solid state based intermediate device.

<u>Possible Choices:</u>

True

False

Answer:

True. Electrohydraulic elevators may have two means to control upward movement, such as pump motor and valve. One or both of these should be controlled by the terminal speed reducing device directly or through an intermediate device implemented via a solid-state device or a software system.

Question 31:

In CT, a certificate of operation for the elevator would be valid for how many months?

Possible Choices:

6

9

12

18

24

Answer:

In CT, a certificate of operation for the elevator would be valid for 12 months.

Question 32:

In CT, the owner of an elevator needs to report to the Department of Public Safety any accident that results in injury or death within:

Possible Choices:

1 hour

2 hours

4 hours

6 hours

8 hours

None of the choices.

Answer:

None of the choices. In CT, the owner of an elevator needs to immediately report to the Department of Public Safety any accident that results in injury or death. The wording is simply "immediately".

Question 1:

Talking about governor rope, tiller-rope construction is always encouraged for reliability.

Possible Choices:

True

False

Answer:

False. A governor rope should be made of iron, steel, or metal no less than 6 mm in diameter. Keep in mind, tiller-rope construction should never be used.

Question 2:

On elevators with a rated load of 230kg or less / speed of 0.15 m/s or less, the suspension ropes should be at least __mm in diameter.

Possible Choices:

4

5

6

7

8

9

11

12

Answer:

On elevators with a rated load of 230kg or less / speed of 0.15 m/s or less, the suspension ropes should be at least 6mm in diameter.

Question 3:

When a car operates via a hatch cover, you should ensure:

Possible Choices:

the counter-weight runway is enclosed throughout its height.

the counter-weight runway is enclosed throughout at least half of its height.

the counter-weight runway is not enclosed throughout its height.

Answer:

When a car operates via a hatch cover, you should ensure the counter-weight runway is enclosed throughout its height.

Question 4:

Driving machines other than hydraulic driving machines should be equipped with brakes that are (choose all that apply):

Possible Choices:

electrically released

mechanically applied

electrically applied

mechanically released

Answer:

Driving machines other than hydraulic driving machines should be equipped with electrically released but mechanically applied brakes.

Question 5:

Elevators for private residence should have a manual operating device:

Possible Choices:

accessible from inside the car .

not accessible from inside the car .

Answer:

Elevators for private residence should allow manual operation during power failure, but the manual operating device should not be accessible from inside the car.

Question 6:

The weight sections of a counter-weight must NOT be mounted in any structural component.

Possible Choices:

True

False

Answer:

False. The weight sections of a counter-weight need to be mounted in a structural metal.

Question 7:

The oil used in the oil buffers of a counter-weight should have a viscosity index of at least:

Possible Choices:

35

50

75

80

85

90

Answer:

The oil used in the oil buffers of a counter-weight should have a viscosity index of at least 75.

Question 8:

On elevators with rated load above 230kg, the suspension ropes should be at least ___mm in diameter.

Possible Choices:

6

7

8

9

12

13

14

Answer:

On elevators with a rated load above 230kg / speed of 0.15 ms, the suspension ropes should be at least 9mm in diameter.

Question 9:

When the driving machine is located on the top of the car,

Possible Choices:

it should be protected by a solid enclosure.

it should NOT be covered so that heat dissipation can be facilitated.

Answer:

When the driving machine is located on the top of the car, it should be protected by a solid and noncombustible enclosure.

Question 10:

Elevators for private residence should have a manual operating device:

Possible Choices:

capable of releasing the brake.

NOT capable of releasing the brake.

Answer:

Elevators for private residence should allow manual operation during power failure, but the manual operating device should not be allowed to release the brake.

Question 11:

Winding drum machines should NOT be equipped with counter-weights.

Possible Choices:

True

False

Answer:

True. Winding drum machines should NOT be equipped with counter-weights.

Question 12:

Elevators that use hydraulic driving machines:

Possible Choices:

should be equipped with a manual lowering valve.

should NOT use manual lowering valve.

Answer:

Elevators that use hydraulic driving machines should be equipped with a manual lowering valve.

Question 13:

When servicing speed governors, the means of speed adjustment should NEVER be sealed.

Possible Choices:

True

False

Answer:

False. When servicing speed governors, make sure the means of speed adjustment are sealed after test.

Question 14:

The bearing and rubbing surfaces of the speed governors:

Possible Choices:

should be painted and coated.

should remain freed of paint.

Answer:

When speed governors are painted, all bearing and rubbing surfaces should remain freed of paint.

Question 15:

Auxiliary rope fastening devices should have a strength which is:

Possible Choices:

at least equal to the manufacturer's breaking strength of the rope to which it is attached.

at least equal to 1.5 times the manufacturer's breaking strength of the rope to which it is attached.

at least equal to 3 times the manufacturer's breaking strength of the rope to which it is attached.

Answer:

Auxiliary rope fastening devices should have a strength which is at least equal to the manufacturer's breaking strength of the rope to which it is attached.

Question 16:

When an elevator car stays outside the unlocking zone, the car doors should not be opened more than _____ mm from within the inside of the car.

<u>Possible Choices:</u>

100

120

150

160

180

200

220

Answer:

When an elevator car stays outside the unlocking zone, the car doors should not be opened more than 100 mm from within the inside of the car.

Question 17:

Suspended glass that is used in an elevator's lighting fixture should be supported by a metal frame secured at least:

Possible Choices:

2 points.

3 points.

5 points.

6 points.

8 points.

Answer:

Suspended glass that is used in an elevator's lighting fixture should be supported by a metal frame, that this frame needs to be secured at least 3 points.

Question 18:

Auxiliary rope fastening devices should function in a rope movement of no more than:

Possible Choices:

38 mm.

48 mm.

58 mm.

68 mm.

78 mm.

88 mm.

Answer:

Auxiliary rope fastening devices should function in a rope movement of no more than 38 mm.

Question 19:

When an elevator car stays inside the unlocking zone, the car doors should be openable from:

Possible Choices:

within the inside of the car.

only the outside of the car.

only the car top.

Answer:

True. When an elevator car stays inside the unlocking zone, the car doors should be openable from within the inside of the car.

Question 20:

You need to have a capacity plate located in a position:

Possible Choices:

inside an elevator car.

outside an elevator car.

only in the control room.

Answer:

False. You need to have a capacity plate located in a conspicuous position inside an elevator car. This plate should indicate the rated load.

Question 21:

Freight elevators may carry passengers.

Possible Choices:

True

False

Answer:

True. Freight elevators may carry passengers. However, they should not be made accessible to the general public.

Question 22:

Any collapsible car gates should not be allowed to power-open to a distance more than:

Possible Choices:

50 mm.

80 mm.

100 mm.

120 mm.

150 mm.

250 mm.

Answer:

Any collapsible car gates should not be allowed to power-open to a distance more than 250 mm.

Question 23:

A three-position key-operated switch for fire operation should include:

Possible Choices:

"OFF," "HOLD," and "ON"

"OFF," "RESET," and "ON"

"UP," "HOLD," and "DOWN"

"OFF," "STOP," and "ON"

Answer:

A three-position key-operated switch for fire operation should include "OFF," "HOLD," and "ON" in that order.

Question 24:

"FIRE RECALL" switches must come with audible signaling. Visual signaling is not required.

Possible Choices:

True

False

Answer:

False. "FIRE RECALL" switches when made available should have illuminated visual signal for indicating when Emergency Recall Operation is in effect.

Question 25:

Preventive Maintenance PM is the most efficient way to maintain elevators.

Possible Choices:

True

False

Answer:

Preventive Maintenance PM is the most efficient way to maintain elevators. It can prolong the life of the elevator equipments and minimize dangerous condition.

Question 26:

Visual awareness review is NEVER a desirable inspection method.

Possible Choices:

True

False

Answer:

False. Regular maintenance is required on the elevators. The possible inspection methods are Visual awareness review; Manual inspection and repair; and Mid-used/failed part replacement.

Question 27:

A three-position key-operated switch for fire operation MUST be labeled with lettering in RED only.

Possible Choices:

True

False

Answer:

False. A three-position key-operated switch for fire operation should be labeled with lettering which is in red or in a color that is contrasting with a red background.

Question 28:

Viscosity is a measure of oil:

Possible Choices:

thickness.

humidity.

quality.

grade.

Answer:

Viscosity is an important property of oil. It is a measure of oil thickness.

Question 29:

Substituting preventive maintenance for _____ is always recommended.

Possible Choices:

careful calibration

proper material selection

careful installation

corrective maintenance

Answer:

Preventive Maintenance PM is the most efficient way to maintain elevators. It can prolong the life of the elevator equipments and minimize dangerous condition. Substituting PM for corrective maintenance is always recommended.

Question 30:

Access to the elevator pit is _____ if you need to inspect the car sheaves.

Possible Choices:

often necessary

strictly unnecessary

Answer:

Access to the elevator pit is usually required if you need to inspect car sheaves. You may particularly want to inspect car sheaves for axial movement or wobble.

Question 31:

In CT, a certificate of operation for the elevator should be posted conspicuously:

Possible Choices:

in the car or on the platform of the elevator.

in the machine room.

in the control space.

in the office of the operator.

Answer:

In CT, a certificate of operation for the elevator should be posted conspicuously in the car or on the platform of the elevator.

Question 32:

The ASME A17.2 covers recommended inspection and testing procedures for (choose all that apply):

Possible Choices:

electric elevators

hydraulic elevators

escalators

moving walks

None of the choices.

Answer:

The ASME A17.2 covers recommended inspection and testing procedures for electric and hydraulic elevators, escalators, and moving walks. The ASME A17.3, on the other hand, guides the safe installation, inspection, testing, operation, and/or insurance of existing elevators and escalators.

Question 33:

The ASME A90.1 applies primarily to the manufacture of gravity lifts.

Possible Choices:

True

False

Answer:

False. The ASME A90.1 applies primarily to the manufacture, installation, maintenance, inspection, and operation of manlifts. It does not cover moving stairways nor gravity lifts.

Question 34:

In CT, one has to serve at least how many years as an R-2 or R-6 journeyperson in order to qualify for the R-5 examination?

Possible Choices:

1

2

3

4

5

None of the choices.

Answer:

In CT, one has to serve at least two years as an R-2 or R-6 journeyperson (or equivalent) in order to qualify for the R-5 examination.

Question 35:

In CT, one has to complete a _____-hour elevator apprenticeship program in order to qualify for the R-2 examination.

Possible Choices:

2000

3000

4000

6000

None of the choices.

Answer:

In CT, one has to complete a two year, 4000-hour elevator apprenticeship program in order to qualify for the R-2 examination

Question 36:

In CT, elevator work licenses are valid for 2 years.

Possible Choices:

True

False

Answer:

False. In CT, elevator work licenses expire every year on August 31st.

Question 1:

Position indicators must have a minimum character height of:

Possible Choices:

1 inch

1.5 inches

2 inches

2.5 inches

3 inches

Answer:

Position indicators are required for all elevator cars, with a minimum character height of 2 inches, and with Illumination of each floor level that is passed or stopped at.

Question 2:

Two-way means of emergency communication in elevator cars for direct communication with authorized personnel:

Possible Choices:

is optional.

is required and must be automatic.

is required and must allow activation by a push button.

is required and may be implemented as handsets or open channel.

Answer:

Two-way means of emergency communication in elevator cars for direct communication with authorized personnel is required. It must allow activation by a push button. Handsets and closed compartments are NOT allowed.

Question 3:

Private residence elevators:

Possible Choices:

are allowed inside a residential dwelling unit

are allowed in a multiple dwelling unit facility

are allowed as a means of access to one single private residence only

all of these are correct

Answer:

Private residence elevators are allowed inside a residential dwelling unit or in a multiple dwelling unit facility as a means of access to one single private residence.

Question 4:

In the case of platform lifts, attendant operation:

Possible Choices:

is allowed by the ASME Standard but is prohibited by the ADA Standard.

is allowed by the ASME Standard and also the ADA Standard.

is not allowed by the ASME Standard but the ADA Standard.

is never allowed.

Answer:

Platform lifts must allow unassisted entry and exit from the lift. Attendant operation is allowed by the ASME A18.1 Standard but is prohibited by the ADA Standards.

Question 5:

The initial opening time of doors has to be ___ seconds minimum.

Possible Choices:

1.5

2

3

4

6

8

Answer:

The initial opening time of doors has to be 3 seconds minimum and cannot be stopped/reduced by user activation of door close.

Question 6:

Audible and visible signals that are required for elevators:

Possible Choices:

have to function automatically at all times.

must allow activation by a push button.

may be implemented as handsets or open channel.

Answer:

Audible and visible signals that are required for elevators have to function automatically at all times during the time the elevator is operational.

Question 7:

What device can be used to control large flow of electrical current with smaller current flow?

Possible Choices:

on delay timer

off delay timer

oneoff timer

latch relay

Answer:

A Latching Relay is a relay that is set (ON) or reset (OFF) by the input of a pulse voltage. After the input voltage is interrupted, the relay can still maintain its set or reset condition. The goal is to control large flow of electrical current with smaller current flow. Two coils are used for controlling the relay.

Question 8:

Which of these devices is often used to operate motors for a specified time?

Possible Choices:

on delay timer

off delay timer

oneoff timer

latch relay

megger

Answer:

Off-delay timer is one that is ready to accept the trigger when the input voltage is applied. An output can be energized by applying the trigger. It is often used to operate motors for a specified time.

Question 9:

Which of these devices is often used for measuring resistance?

Possible Choices:

on delay timer

off delay timer

oneoff timer

latch relay

megger

Answer:

We use a "megger" to "meg out" electrical wiring and equipment to find out if it is shorted to ground or the frame in any way. It works by measuring resistance.

Question 10:

Shunts are typically designed for:

Possible Choices:

1/2 of their rated current.

2/3 of their rated current.

3/4 of their rated current.

4/5 of their rated current.

Answer:

Shunts are actually resistors that generates heat. They are typically designed for max of 2/3 their rated current. They may be run in excess of this if the shunt temperature does not exceed 80 degrees C.

Question 11:

Counterweights are for counter balancing the weight of the car plus _____% of the Capacity Load.

Possible Choices:

25%

35%

40%

50%

60%

Answer:

Counterweights are for counter balancing the weight of the car plus 40% of the Capacity Load.

Question 12:

Which of these is not true regarding residential dumbwaiters?

Possible Choices:

normally travel about 20-30 feet per minute.

need to make a minimum of two stops.

should all come with interlocks.

is restricted to max 12 square feet

Answer:

Residential dumbwaiters normally travel about 20-30 feet per minute. They need to make a minimum of two stops. They should all come with interlocks that lock the access doors on all levels that the car is not on.

Question 13:

LULA elevators has a weight capacity limit of:

Possible Choices:

1000lb

1200lb

1400lb

1600lb

1800lb

Answer:

LULA elevators are limited use and limited application. They are limited in weight capacity (max 1400lb), floor space (max 18 square feet) as well as travel distance (max 26ft).

Question 14:

The interaction between wires laid jointly to create a rope:

Possible Choices:

is a form of active redundancy

is a form of passive redundancy

Answer:

While running over the traction sheave and the deflection sheaves, wires ropes are exposed to a high complex of stress factors, including tension, flexural stress, torsion and compression. They may break... Active redundancy can be achieved through the interaction between wires laid jointly to create a rope so that when one component fails the remaining components can still take on its functions.

Question 15:

Safety gear is an example of:

Possible Choices:

active redundancy

passive redundancy

Answer:

While running over the traction sheave and the deflection sheaves, wires ropes are exposed to a high complex of stress factors, including tension, flexural stress, torsion and compression. They may break... Safety gear is an example of passive redundancy.

Question 16:

19-wire Seale strand is a popular strand construction for elevator ropes.

Possible Choices:

True

False

Answer:

True. A popular strand construction for elevator ropes is the 19-wire Seale strand (1-9-9). It has thick outer wires and can offer a higher degree of resistance against external wear.

Question 17:

Governor ropes will engage:

Possible Choices:

the interlock

the door sensor

the on delay timer

the safety gear

the latch relay

Answer:

Governor ropes that run in the moulded groove of the governor pulley will engage the safety gear when an overspeed situation is detected.

Question 18:

A submersible screw pump:

Possible Choices:

can avoid metal-to-metal contact between the rotor and the idlers.

requires metal-to-metal contact between the rotor and the idlers.

requires lubed metal-to-metal contact between the rotor and the idlers.

Answer:

A submersible screw pump that serves as an elevator power unit allows the axial and radial forces on the rotors to be hydraulically balanced and avoid metal-to-metal contact between the rotor and the idlers.

Question 19:

A slack rope valve:

Possible Choices:

is a safety feature

is a control feature

is an optional feature

is a performance feature

Answer:

A slack rope valve is a safety feature of a control valve that is very important in indirect roping installations.

Question 20:

Which of these are the startup methods used by motor for a hydraulic elevator (choose all that apply)?

Possible Choices:

DOL

Star-delta start

Soft-starter start

Fixed-starter delay

Answer:

The motor used for a hydraulic elevator must produce the necessary torque. There are different startup methods but the most common are Direct-on-line start (DOL), Star-delta start and Soft-starter start.

Question 21:

When there are two cylinders that work in tandem,

Possible Choices:

they should share the same rupture valve.

their rupture valves should still remain independent so they do not need to work in tandem.

their rupture valves are connected to each other so they can work in tandem as well.

Answer:

Some elevator installations have two cylinders that work in tandem. There are two rupture valves connected to each other so they can work in tandem.

Question 22:

The rails used with the roller guides:

Possible Choices:

should be kept dry.

should be lubed with oxidized lubricant.

should be lubed, but not with oxidized lubricant.

Answer:

The rails used with the roller guides should be kept dry. On the other hand, the rails must be free of oxidized lubricant in the area where the safety jaws apply.

Question 23:

The governor ropes:

Possible Choices:

should be kept dry.

should be lubricated in the field whenever possible.

should be lubed with oxidized lubricant.

should be lubed, but not with oxidized lubricant.

Answer:

The brake cores and the pivots should be lubricated following manufacturer's specifications. On the other hand, the governor ropes should not be lubricated in the field. It should stay dry.

Question 24:

The up thrust roller to track clearance should not be allowed to exceed:

Possible Choices:

0.15 inches.

0.015 inches.

0.05 inches.

0.510 inches.

0.615 inches.

Answer:

Up thrusts should be bale to prevent the doors from jumping the track. The up thrust roller to track clearance should not be allowed to exceed 0.015 inches.

Question 25:

The car door closing force must not exceed:

Possible Choices:

20 lb.

25 lb.

30 lb.

35 lb.

40 lb.

50 lb.

Answer:

The door system masses must be considered when you adjust the door closing speed. In any case the door closing force must not exceed 30 lb.

Question 26:

Pinpoint sparking of the motor:

Possible Choices:

is considered normal during acceleration and stopping.

is considered abnormal during acceleration and stopping.

Answer:

Pinpoint sparking of the motor is considered normal during acceleration and stopping. Severe arcing is NOT!

Question 27:

Using high voltage meggers on elevator electrical equipment:

Possible Choices:

is recommended

is recommended on a weekly basis

is recommended on a quarterly basis

is not recommended

is not allowed

Answer:

Using high voltage meggers or high voltage pulse tests on electrical equipment is not a good idea as insulation damage that cannot be readily detected may result.

Question 28:

In the control system circuitry, wire jumpers:

Possible Choices:

is recommended

is allowed although not recommended

should not be allowed

Answer:

Time delay fuses may be used only in the circuits where specified. Renewable link fuses are never recommended, and that wire jumpers must not be allowed.

Question 29:

Spring buffer is often found on elevators with speeds less than _____ feet per minute.

Possible Choices:

100

120

150

200

300

400

Answer:

A spring buffer aims to prevent the bottom of the cabin from crashing hard on the floor. It is often found on elevators with speeds less than 200 feet per minute. Those that are faster may use oil buffer instead.

END OF BOOK

Made in United States
North Haven, CT
18 September 2022

24267469R00089